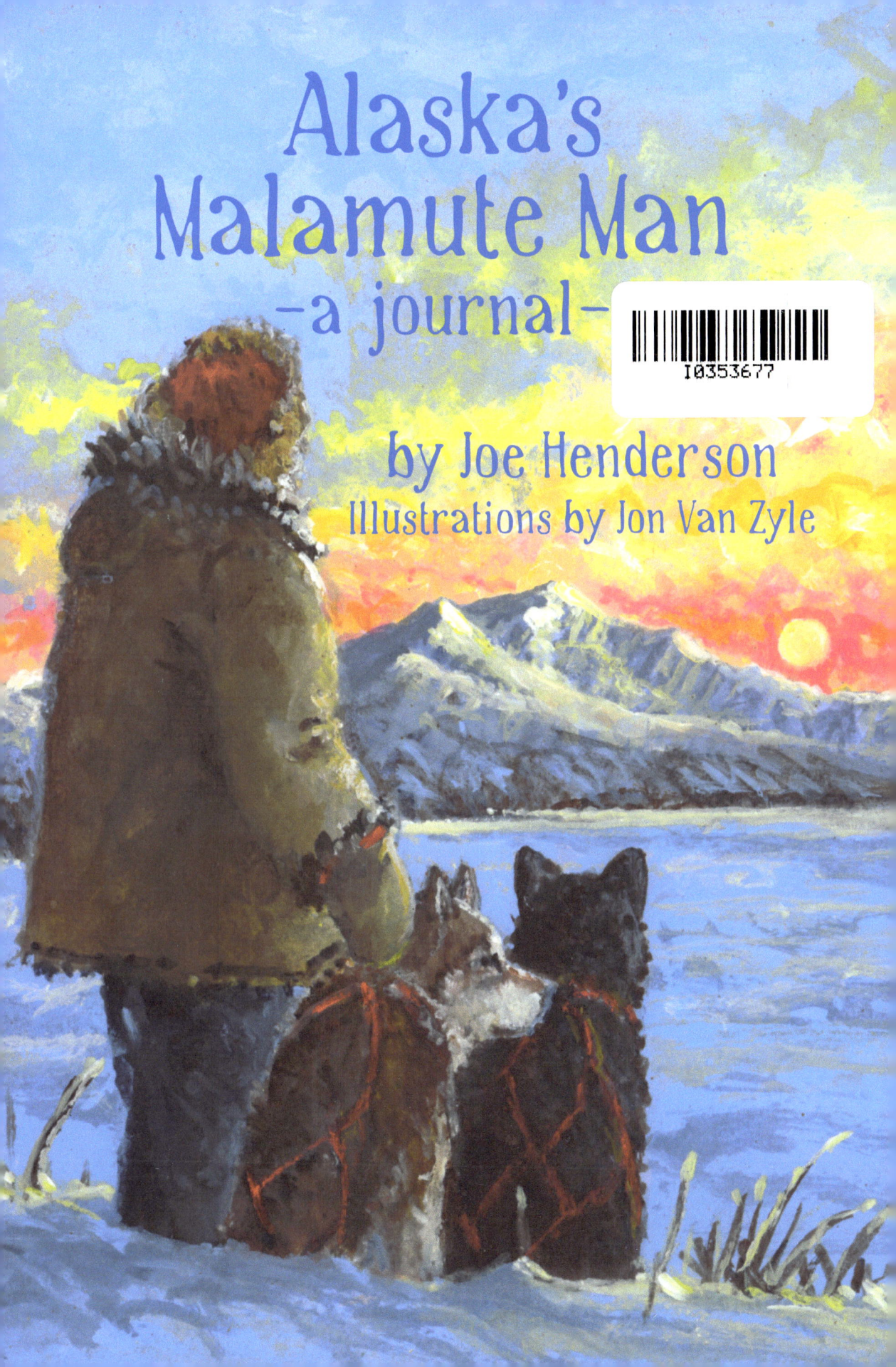

Alaska's Malamute Man
—a journal—

by Joe Henderson

Illustrations by Jon Van Zyle

Epicenter Press

6524 NE 181st St., Suite 2, Kenmore, WA 98028

Epicenter Press is a regional press publishing nonfiction books about the arts, history, environment, and diverse cultures and lifestyles of Alaska and the Pacific Northwest. For more information, visit www.EpicenterPress.com

Copyright © 2022 by Joe Henderson

All rights reserved. No part of this publication may be reproduced, stored in a retrieval system, or transmitted in any form by any means, electronic, mechanical, photocopying, recording, or otherwise, without the prior written permission of the publisher. Permission is given for brief excerpts to be published with book reviews in newspaper, magazines, newsletters, catalogs, and online publications.

ISBN: 978-1-684920-00-6 (Trade Paperback)
ISBN: 978-1-68492-001-3 (Ebook)

Printed in the United States of America

Illustrations by Jon Van Zyle

*To our merciful Lord Jesus Christ who has given me
strength and opportunity to experience and share
my adventures in the hope to inspire others.*

—Joe Henderson

*For all of us who treasure the Arctic lands . . . To those of us
that have been fortunate to share our journeys with our dog
teams, and to those who dream of such an adventure,
I dedicate my art and Joe's words*

—Jon Van Zyle

1-24-14

Now, at the eve of another Arctic expedition, deep snow has transformed the landscape into an Angel-white, clean, and fresh winter-land. Outside my log cabin, which is nestled in a deep forest by the town of North Pole Alaska, the mournful and yearning sounds of my malamutes howling into the night is echoing through the forest. Inside, it's warm and aglow with golden candlelight, and the sweet aroma of wood-smoke mingled with fresh coffee brewing is lingering in the air. It's 2 a.m., and both the dogs and I are anxiously waiting for dawn.

Day 1, 1-25-14

We have arrived at our Arctic expedition base camp.

As I stand on the edge of a destitute no-man's land, viewing the white expanse of windswept hills and jagged mountains, I feel like a burden has been lifted off my shoulders and my spirit is set free. I have returned to the land that I love and hate, dread and cherish. I know that the ravages of a brutal and unforgiving Arctic winter await me. I have returned nonetheless, to do what I was born to do.

. . . while the blood red sun shaves the mountain peaks momentarily and then sinks below the horizon, the dogs lift their muzzles toward the dark blue sky and howl a tune that stirs all the Angels in heaven. . . the malamutes have returned to their ancestral homeland.

Last night, under the lamp's yellow glow, I unfolded the map of Alaska's Brooks Range, and searched for an area with brutally broken and rugged terrain, wide open braided river valleys, and majestic towering peaks that scraped the heavens. I want to see a wild land, free of human intrusion, a place that is so damned inaccessible and forbidden that only wolves and eagles visit. Instinctively, I know in my mind's eye what I am searching for. Like an artist that visualizes his finished piece of work before he picks-up brush and paint, I imagine the majestic landscape waiting at our destination. I believe what I do is an art, and similar to artists, I must entertain my passion. But the finished piece of art is insignificant-it's the process of which it is created that is most important. It's about the story, the road, the trials and triumphs, the winding trail where we are led during our pursuit of creating the masterpiece.

Day 2, +25°F

Today, I broke trail ahead of the dogteam across the river. It was dangerously thin ice but we managed to cross without incident. We're camped on a hillside that overlooks a broad valley that falls away to high rolling hills with small patches of willow scattered about protruding from the windswept snow. Ahead of us, is a low pass that leads to a winding valley. I hope to follow this river valley to its headwaters, and then ascend a steep pass that leads to a broad twisted valley where majestic, spiraled peaks dominate the blue.

The willow brush is too small for firewood so I'll conserve burning the stove tonight. The clean fresh Arctic air and open expanse is exhilarating! I thought about calling a friend and family member but the phone is my only means of communication so I better conserve the batteries in case of emergency.

Day 3, 14 +12°F

Last night, the Northern Lights streamed and danced overhead like a lively spirit being set free. For a moment she awoke the heavens in a magnificent display of brilliant colors of greens, purples, and shaded yellows, working the sky like an artist's fine brush with patterns that resembled ocean waves crashing against the reefs . . . and then she sighed, flickered, and succumbed to the black night.

Day 4 +15°F

The team is working together like a fine-tuned orchestra with each team member complimenting the other. When a dog steps in a deep hole and stumbles, the dog beside him pulls vigorously until his running mate regains his composure. They are thinking, pulling, breaking trail as one cumulative unit of flesh, bone, and muscle.

Without a fire in the heart passion to pull, the dogs are nothing more than machines, robots, wage slaves. Like people, they have hidden desires in their hearts that are ready to ignite. All they need is a spark. I provide the spark and they supply the fire.

When both an animal and a person recognize that their survival depends on each other there is no longer a dominate role of either person or animal. They work and live together as one unit. Emotions are felt between them like they are one being. When one suffers or feels joy so does the other.

Day 5

As the sleds gently slid down the mountain pass toward the river valley my heart sank. Ahead of us, hovering above the valley, a grey cloud of steam and vapor darkened my hopes of traveling on the river. As we got closer to the river, rushing sounds of water crushed the peaceful silence. My planned route is obliterated. The water is most likely flowing from thermal springs and hasn't frozen yet because of these damned unseasonably mild temperatures. Now, we are forced to travel an alternative route which will lead us across the open and windy flats, to an awful area of continuous rolling hills, deep snow, creeks aligned with tangled willow brush, canyons, and mountain crevasses. Thus is life, thus is art.

Day 6 +20°F

It seems that all day we climbed higher and higher in elevation. The rolling hills amidst the white expanse are numbing my depth perception and senses. It's like traveling in a perpetual white cloud of nothingness- an endless blinding white that leads to the edge of earth. My thigh muscles burn from continuously climbing, and the dogs are pulling with everything they got, but soon we will travel in the mountains where the towering peaks will cast shadows on our backs, humbling our souls with its majestic beauty.

Day 7 +20°F

When I lash on my snowshoes, the team follows me with childlike faith and hearts of courage. Although there are not trails or defined routes to guide me, the dogs trust that I will lead them safely through one of the most hostile environments on the planet. Canyons, crevasses, cliffs, thin ice on rivers, and avalanches await us, but I also travel with blind faith knowing that the Lord will lead me. It's the essence and art of exploring. It captivates your spirit and forces you to rely on your instincts, creativity, and faith.

Day 8 +20°F

Now, the sun rises above the horizon a few hours. She still doesn't offer any warmth but her blood red glow strikes the malamutes' coats like flames of fire. We crossed a large teardrop shaped lake which provided my legs a break from struggling up the hills. The dogs seemed to enjoy the short and sweet break on the level lake-ice surface as well.

Day 9 +27°F

It snowed heavily today. Miserable wet, despicable snow. My clothing is wet, I am chilled to the bone, exhausted, and my sleeping bag is so damn cold and clammy that I can't sleep. I don't know the time, but its black as sin outside and the moon has hidden his silver smile. But inside the tent, inside my green canvas pack, are a few items that I never travel without which seems to soothe my soul on restlessness nights: a soft red checkered scarf that my daughter had given me for Christmas many, many years ago, photographs of my children and grandchildren, a letter from an old friend, and the Bible.

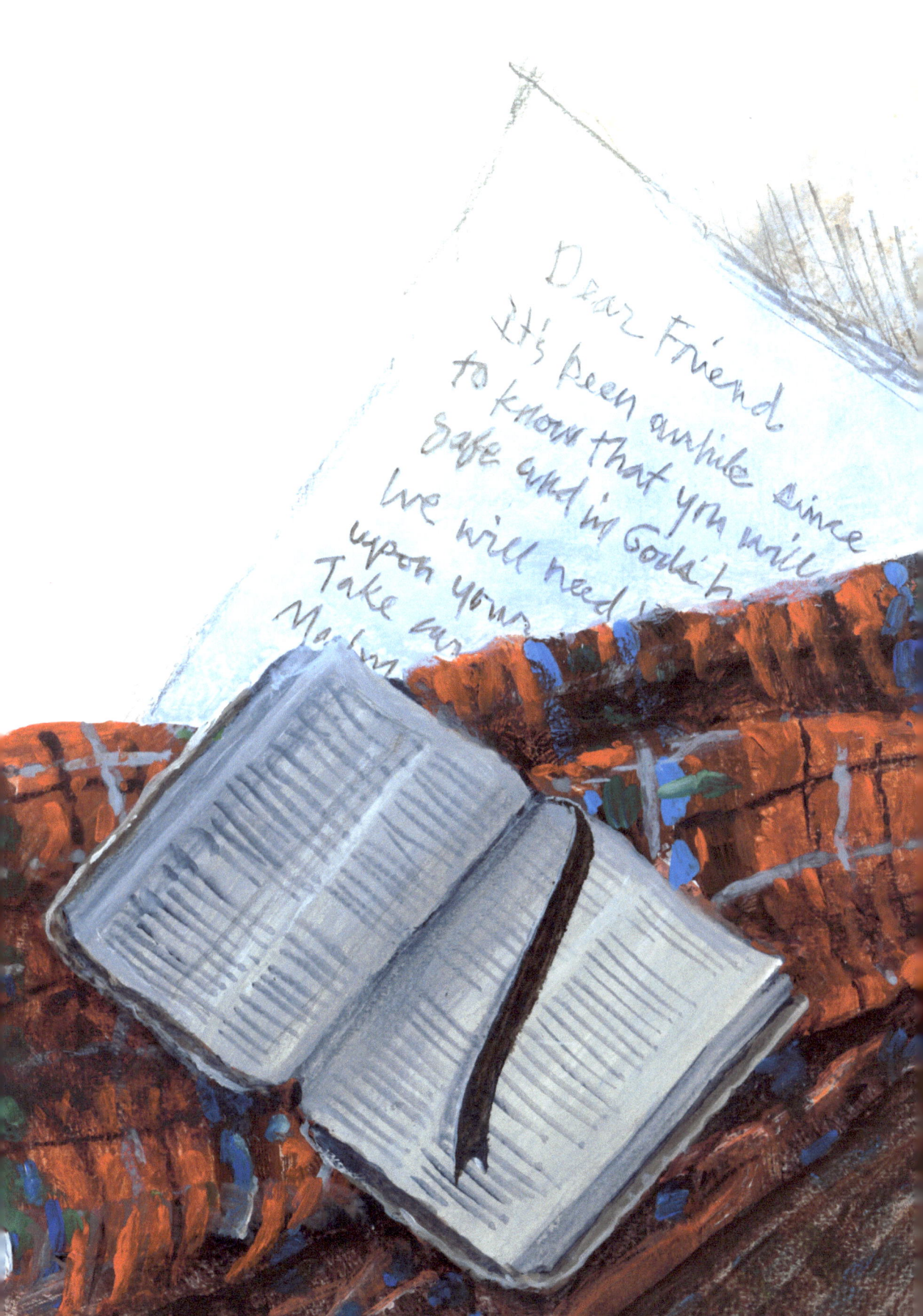

Day 10 -5°F

Today, the team pulled 2,000 lb of freight up the pass while breaking trail. Now, the team's concerted strength is cemented into their psych . . .

. . . Training freighters is mostly psychological. Once they believe their strength is invincible-almost nothing can stop them . . . .

When a dog discovers that his strength has a limit. He will accept this limit as the peak of his strength. But if he does not know his limit, and he has never discovered it, then he will reach deep within his soul and spirit and exhibit feats of strength which is beyond human comprehension. And then, when 22 dogs are combined into a team, all of which do not know their limits of strength, the team can conquer what has been claimed to be impossible.

Day 11

We are camped beside a large, windswept lake on the summit. On both sides of us are mountains shaped like great pyramids of Egypt. On the horizon, is a low hallow which will take us to a narrow valley, where I hope to gather willow brush to replenish my firewood supply. Trees are extremely rare in the Arctic. So, dry willow is my only source of fuel for cooking and heat. Something strange and mysterious is in the air. I have an uneasy feeling. It doesn't make sense. There's an aroma in the breeze, like willow buds and grasses during springtime, but it's not spring-its dead of winter. My gut instincts are warning me that something terrible is coming . . . .

The wind has shifted now, and coming from the south . . .

. . . it sounded like the gates of hell busted open tonight. Hurricane force winds swept across the tundra, pushing a tidal wave of snow that obliterated and buried everything in her path. The tent shook and shuttered, creaked and moaned, the candle flame flickered, cowered, and then a cold powdery mist of snow settled on me and my fur sleeping mats . . .

. . . I grabbed my mukluks, parka, and gloves, slipped them on, and rushed out the door. The eye stinging snow impaired visibility to a few feet and the cold wind pierced through my clothing like I was naked. Quickly, I piled the harnesses and other loose gear on top of the sleds, lashed them down, checked the dogs, reassured the rookies that they would survive, grabbed my shovel, and crawled inside the tent . . . .

Day 12 -96°F wind-chill

The blizzard is still raging, tearing, and stripping life's peace apart . . . .

The horrendous sounds are muffled now. The tent is entombed in a layer of drifted snow. The dogs are doing fine, especially the veterans that have allowed themselves to be buried under a soft, warm, blanket of drifted snow. They're resting comfortably now. The rookies however, spent much of last night playing, howling and whining, just as youngsters do . . .

The wind-chill has dropped to -96°F. The young dogs have decided to follow the veterans' wise strategy. They've allowed themselves to be covered with a warm blanket of snow.

... The blizzard, I hate. She is pure hell on earth. She beats you, freezes you, confuses your senses, and rips your exposed flesh with her devious sharp fangs of frost. She crushes your soul with loneliness and boredom while you wait in your dark canvas adobe for her to exhale her last breath. Yet she is a friend and savior who sweeps away the soft deep snow, transforming it into hard pack which allows us to travel across the land with relative ease ...

Day 14 -45°F

Although the fresh air is invigorating and cleansing to the body, it can bite you like a deadly snake. You must move swiftly at all times to prevent frostbite from tearing your flesh. Frostbite is a nagging reminder who governs the Arctic.

Day 15

The blizzard has fallen away. She has exhausted her last vital sign of life. It's time to stretch my legs and hit the trail . . .

We crossed the lake and descended the pass, and now, the team is resting with well fed bulging tummies. The wood-burning stove is crackling and glowing apple red, and the appetizing aroma of cooked moose-meat, tallow, and rice is lingering in the air. My ration of peanut butter and honey is in two separate plastic containers thawing beside the stove, and the large slice of white cheese is looking awfully palatable now. Thus are the simple pleasure in life.

Day 16

Damn, she is back! 50 mph winds tore down the valley, whipping snow in our faces and reduced visibility to a few feet. It's painful when you are traveling against a wind that whips and antagonizes your existence.

Day 17 -50°F

Its calm and clear and the snow is becoming dry as sand. We are now struggling to travel ten miles a day. The terrain is deviously steep and rugged with creeks, and hillsides covered heavily with twisted webs of willow brush.

Day 18 -65°F wind-chill

Another blizzard swept through and pinned me down for another day. These blizzards are killing me. Thankfully though, the blizzard struck as we were crossing a creek where the snow was drifted deep. The deep snow allows me to dig down a meter or so, and then set the tent over the hole I've made. This way, I am protected from the wind's force since I am beneath the snow surface.

Time and supplies are running low. I've proportioned myself a strict ration of meat, rice, cheese, peanut butter, honey, and coffee. But the dogs are allowed a generous amount of dogfood and oils. It's always my goal that they gain weight during an expedition-it's part of the psychological training that enables them to stay in high spirits every year. But we can't be forced to sit idle any longer. Hell or high water we will travel tomorrow.

Day 19 -45°F

Temperatures are plummeting and the dry snow is becoming worst. Please God-give us fresh snow!

Day 20 -72°F wind-chill

The grinding sounds of the runners against the dry snow are deafening. The team is pulling with all their hearts, my thigh muscles and tendons are burning sore, and my hands are stiff and crippled from gripping, pushing, and pulling the sled . . . where is the fresh snow!

Day 21 -72°F wind-chill

. . . Why God do I subject myself to this brutality . . . why am I constantly reminded me of my pain and suffering?

I must mimic my malamute comrades . . . they are all working with relish like cheerful warriors . . . why can't I endure like them? I must, and I will.

Day 22 -53°F

. . . I know the finish line is sweet and full. I must keep pushing myself, driving my body forward, one step at a time, pushing, pulling, dragging, breaking trail. I must go onward and never give up . . .

As I reflect on the expedition, my favorite proverb comes to mind: "There is that who makes himself rich yet has nothing, there is that who makes himself poor, but has great riches."

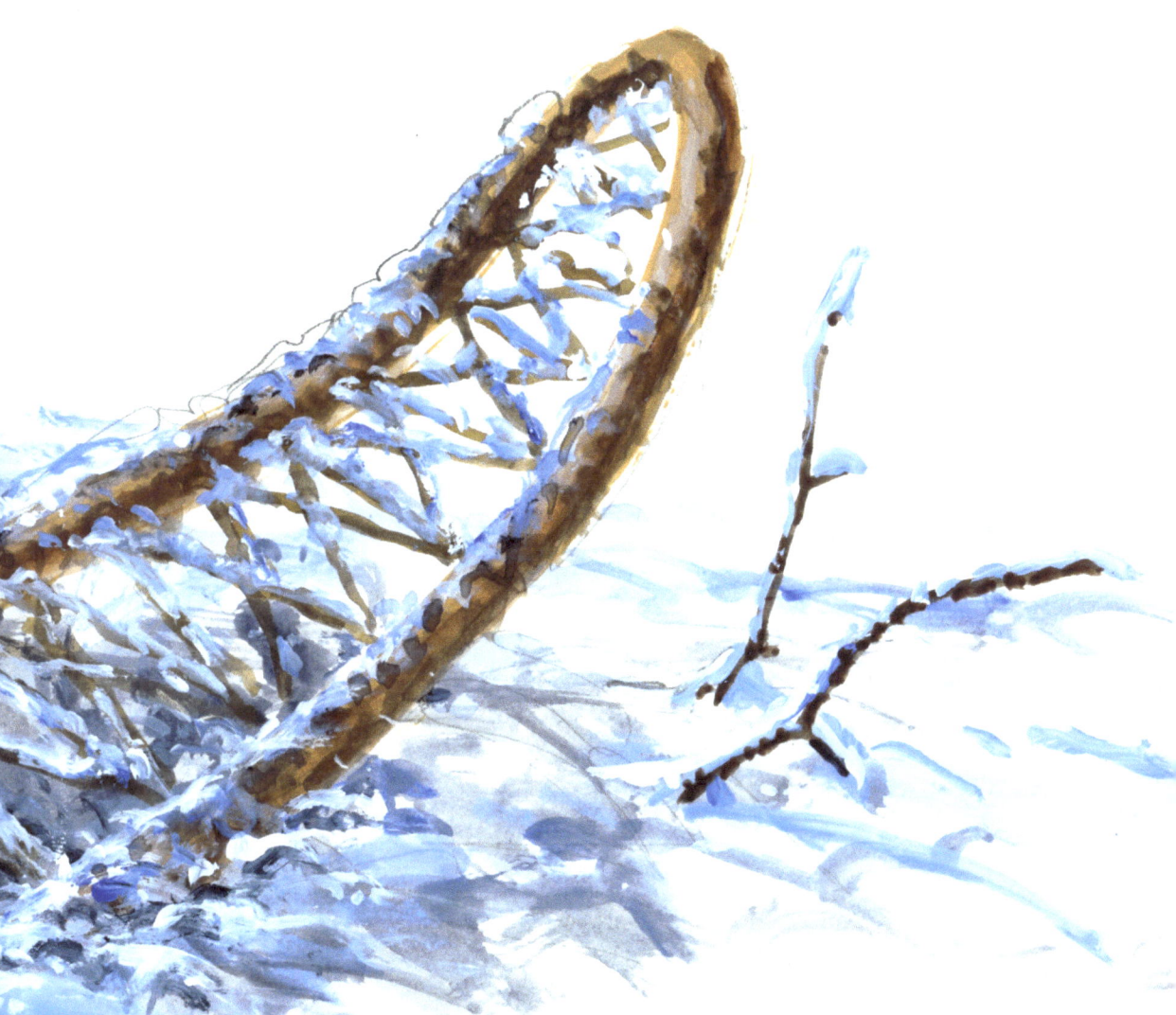

Day 23 -52°F

The brutal bastardly cold is killing me. Every day we struggle in the driest, sandiest, most miserable, son-of-bitching, snow I've ever seen. The sleds drag, screech, resist, and rebel. I push and the dogs pull. The dogs will never yield. I will never give up . . . .

The darkness of suffering has entombed me but my soul is lifted by the fire's brightness that is illuminating my comrades by my side. Their loyalty, love and adoration for me rejuvenates my spirit. Even though the trail has been a hard-fought battle, I know in my heart with relished gladness, I will have the strength to continue and give my malamutes the opportunity to do what they love and are born to do. I also realize that this battle is only one page of my life and there are many more pages and chapters to be lived that will bring me joy.

Day 24 -35°F

It's over . . . for now.

I've pushed my miserable human body as far as it will go. My limbs feel like lead weights, I am weak as sin, my heart is banging my chest, and my nose is bleeding from exhaustion . . . I will survive. I will rest. And then I will march on.

Day 25

I have been consuming 10,000 calories a day and yet, I am losing weight. My body will adjust. The son-of-a-bitch doesn't have a choice.

When I glimpse behind the team and see the winding trail we've made, the twists and turns over mountain passes and wide braided river valleys that disappear on the horizon, I am awestruck in the vastness of God's creation. Many times, the team and I have traveled in the rugged mountain regions for four to five months and had never seen another human being or signs of human activity, most likely because it is a desolate lonely land, painfully cold, dark as sin in winter, and outright unfriendly to human beings.

Countless times, I have been battered by hurricane-force winds with -100°F wind-chill, charged by crazed grizzly bears, broken through thin ice, nearly drowned, and have felt the fangs of cold so deep in my marrow that I thought I'd never see another sunrise. But by the grace of God, and drawing on his strength, the team and I have managed to survive while breaking trail forward, extending that never-ending trail behind us. Our reward is the opportunity to explore the Arctic's precious gem of an untouched wilderness and experiencing the tranquility and peace that comes along with it.

Day 26 -50°F

A God-awful barren land lies before me. The wind is like small knives cutting my flesh as I struggle forward on legs that are fatigued with burning muscles, and lungs that feel like they are going to explode. I dare not stop. Nope, I must keep moving swiftly, quickly, methodically, yet not too fast, otherwise the sweat will seep from my pours, freeze to

ice, and allow my enemy, hypothermia, to kill me. No, I know better than that–I've walked this tight rope many times. Just one slip, one screw-up, and I'm a dead man. And then the dogs would be next. They would not have a chance in hell to survive. They would be torn to shreds by the wolves that have been following us . . .

Day 27 -72°F wind-chill

Dry, dry snow. Ever so damn dry and slow traveling. We only average ½ mph. On a good day we average 1 mph. The valley has opened wide and its viciously windy. The hills are behind us now but the continuous waist deep and dry snow is tearing my spirit to pieces. My heart is distressed and discouraged, and seeds of doubt are planting their miserable selves in my mind. But I rebuke those cowardly thoughts. They are devious and sly, and I will not fall as their prey. The team is in high spirits. I will mimic the dogs-we will march on.

Day 29 -50°F wind-chill

Thoughts of doubt and self-imposed limits are like heavy anchors. They drag you down to a powerless being, suppressing creativity and relinquishes your fight to succeed and survive. They are venomous malignant thoughts. If allowed, they will prosper and grow and kill your spirit's strength.

Day 30

The Arctic doesn't take prisoners. Either she embraces you or she spits you out, slowly killing you. Today, while searching for dry willow brush to burn, I come upon a wretched old dead porcupine, frozen stiff, skinny, and frail. Porcupines are rare in Alaska's Arctic and now, they are very rare. Obviously, succumbed to the extreme temperatures, the beast had very little chance to live. Often, you wonder how any life exists in one of the most barbarous environments known to mankind.

Day 32 -50°F

Now, I'm camped in a low hallow surrounded by thick willow. The silver moon is casting its glow on the dogs curled tight and sleeping comfortably in the deep soft snow. I fear though, the two wolves, one black as sin and the other grey, that followed us today have ill intentions. I will sleep with my rifle tonight, in my sleeping bag, and ready to defend my dogs if they attack.

We are surrounded by towering mountains that seem like they are protecting their fortress with sharp spear shaped peaks. And the snow is becoming deeper, and deeper as we climb elevation.

Day 34

Now, snow conditions have become the worst I have ever seen. It's waist deep, which is difficult in itself, but there is a layer of ice beneath the powder snow that collapses under the dogs' weight. The dogs are struggling and punching through the hard layer with each step. Our pace is slow and tedious, and my snowshoes are wearing thin from the abrasive snow. But the sight of raw and rugged mountains piercing the clouds moves and invigorates my body and spirit. We'll march on.

Day 35

Progress is a slow methodical struggle.

Day 36

It's Pete's first year in harness, three years old, and he's showing an extraordinary talent and athletic ability to navigate through these miserable snow conditions.

Day 37

Today, Pete's fire in the heart passion has been ignited and now its burning hot. He's beside Farmer breaking trail with gusto. So, I've taken Junior from lead and placed him in wheel where he feels more comfortable and the work is tough and steady. Now, his brushy red tail is curled with pride and pleasure while he's wearing a perpetual grin.

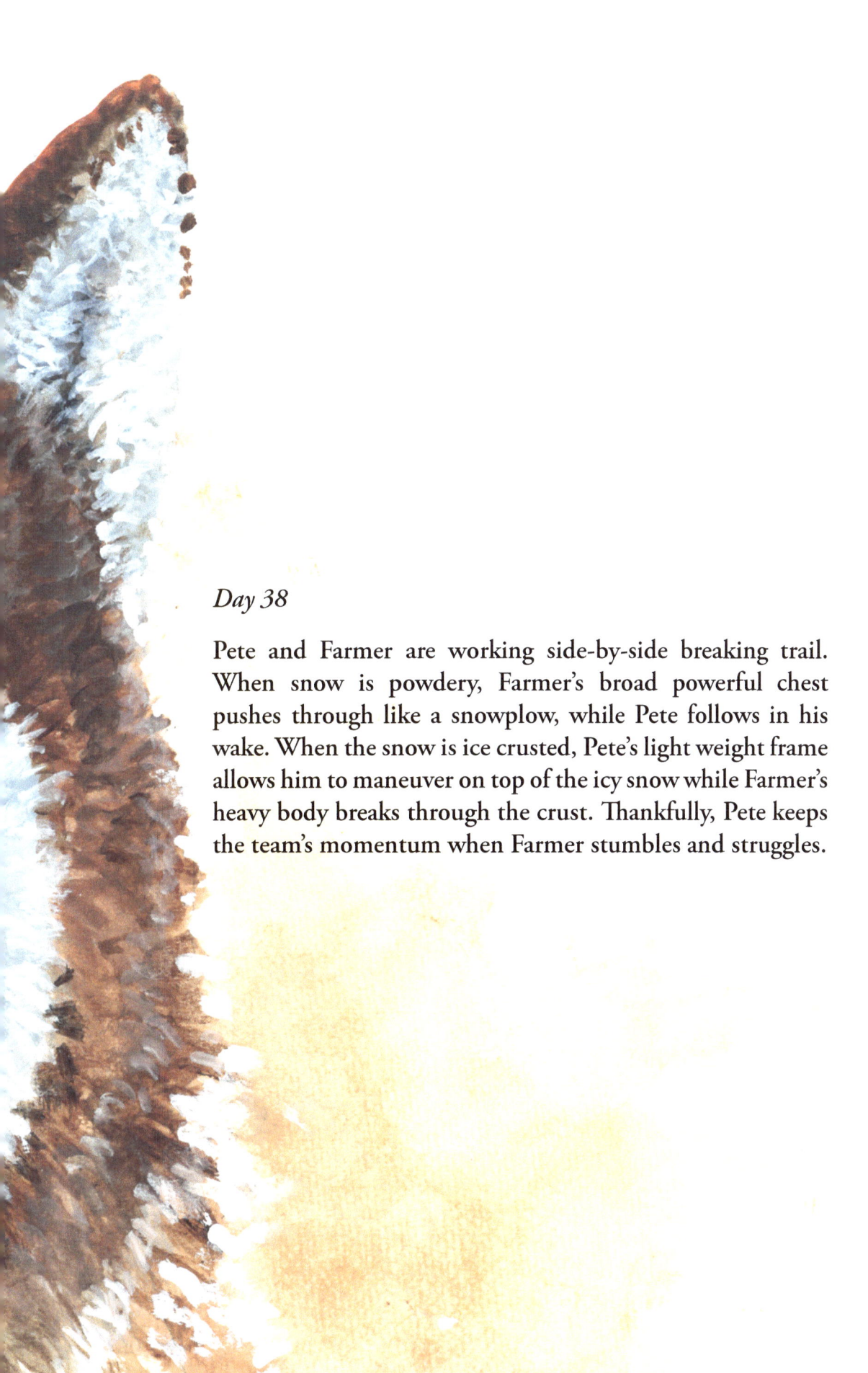

Day 38

Pete and Farmer are working side-by-side breaking trail. When snow is powdery, Farmer's broad powerful chest pushes through like a snowplow, while Pete follows in his wake. When the snow is ice crusted, Pete's light weight frame allows him to maneuver on top of the icy snow while Farmer's heavy body breaks through the crust. Thankfully, Pete keeps the team's momentum when Farmer stumbles and struggles.

Day 39 -40°F

Now, my body has complied to the rigorous demands the environment has placed upon it. It's lean and tireless. It refuses to weaken at the heavy hand of labor. Every day is like running a marathon wearing snowshoes. Fifteen hours a day, I am working: breaking camp, harnessing dogs, snowshoeing, skiing, pushing and shoving, pulling and lifting. The work is endless, gratifying, and breathes enthusiasm and health into my soul. Nothing can stop us now.

A dog's iron will and a person's spirit combined is a formidable force. They become one team, one being, one cohesive unit working together to overcome what was believed to be impossible.

Day 41 -50°F wind-chill

The twisted river valley has now forced us into a gorge choked with thick brush. It will take three days to work through it. We are running low on supplies . . . hell or high water we will keep trudging forward.

Day 42

I'm awestruck watching Farmer break trail in this snow. He slaps the snow, shattering the hard layer on top and then plows through it.

Day 43 -10°F

Tonight, while camping beside a trickling stream, I'm settled on my sled of dwindling supplies of groceries and dogfood and carefully studying the two mountains that are casting their cold shadows on me. The jagged shadows have led my eyes up the slope to a low saddle between them. To the right of the saddle, lay a twisted creek valley that cuts through a boulder strewn canyon as it winds up the mountainside. According to my map, this twisted creek leads to a large lake. I'm thinking, if we climb the steep slope, cross the lake, and continue over the mountain pass, we will descend, and then find ourselves at the doorstep of my goal.

Day 45 +25°F

Unseasonably warm today. The sled runners were deafening silent on the wet snow as they slid effortlessly across the perpetual white landscape . . . .

The willows were beginning to bud in the intense sunlight today.

As we climbed, the mountains looked intimidating. Strangely, they seemed to welcome us . . . it felt like they were alive, gently exhaling a gentle breeze that smelled like green willows and grasses.

Day 46 +10°F

When I led the team up the steep slope I felt insignificant amongst those towering giant reminders of our mortality . . .

Day 48 +30°F

The dogs are pulling with every muscle fiber in their bodies and are in high spirits . . . son-of-a-bitch! We're going to make it!

Day 49 +30°F

Three wolves sat on their haunches, howling an ever so familiar ancient song as the team came to a halt beside a wide windswept river. The malamutes chimed in with perfect harmony as though their beautiful tunes were rehearsed.

Day 51 +30°F

Now, as I sit on sled which is nearly empty of supplies and looking up at those towering peaks scraping the heavens, strangely they seem to be looking down on me with a twisted grin of pride. Here I am a beaten, exhausted, wreck of a man. The clothing that is clinging to me is dirty, torn and worn thin. My straggled hair and beard, I am sure, is an awful sight. Yet, I am reinvigorated. My soul and mind feel cleansed and refreshed with the somber realization how this brutal, cruel, cursed and cussed environment is also sweet with riches that humble the hardy souls that respect her and are willing to sacrifice and pay the price to be in her presence.

The Arctic is an unforgiving place that commands deep respect. You cannot conquer her or plant flags into her soils and claim it as your own. She does not succumb to society's restraints on freedom. She has her own spirit and governs the land how she chooses and rewards or punishes whom she wishes. And those who venture onto her frozen soils will either heed to her demands or become a frozen part of her landscape where the Arctic wolves urinate.

Day 52 +10°F

I hate to turn my back on her. But I must go. My supplies are exhausted, my ribs are showing pathetically through my flesh. But a part of me and the dogs will always remain here, on the tundra, on the mountain peaks, in the crystalline creeks, amongst the sweet-smelling willows, flickering with the stars, and flowing with the cool breezes drifting over the braided river valleys. This land, where we fought, bled, struggled, suffered, laughed with joy, and inspired from God's immense creation has become part of us. It breathes our spirits and souls.

Day 68

We have successfully returned to base camp.

Now, Farmer and the team have their muzzles raised toward heaven, howling an ancient tune that echoes to the ends of the earth.

Ordinary dogs have accomplished extraordinary things because they didn't know they couldn't.

www.ingramcontent.com/pod-product-compliance
Lightning Source LLC
Chambersburg PA
CBHW041109070526
44583CB00003B/123